Presented to:

_____

Presented by:

_____

Date:

_____

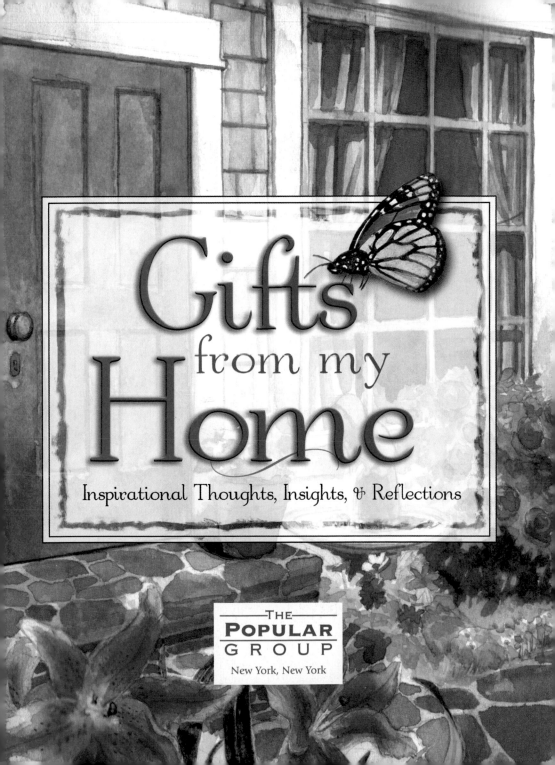

Gifts from my Home

Inspirational Thoughts, Insights, & Reflections

THE
POPULAR
GROUP
New York, New York

Gifts from My Home
ISBN 1-59027-048-7

Copyright © 2002 by GRQ Ink, Inc.
1948 Green Hills Blvd.
Franklin, Tennessee 37067

Published by **Popular Publishing Company, LLC**
3 Park Avenue
New York, New York 10016

Developed by GRQ Ink, Inc.
Cover and text design by Whisner Design Group, Tulsa, Oklahoma
Illustrations by Stephen Gilpin, Tulsa, Oklahoma
Text written by Harriet E. Crosby

Ironing

I have a confession to make: I love to iron. I love the smell of starch as I spray my clothes and the mist of steam as it wafts from the iron. I especially enjoy ironing tablecloths and napkins, starching them stiffly, carefully pressing each fold in the fabric. In a small way, ironing is bringing order out of chaos, beauty out of confusion.

There's another thing I love about ironing. While I iron away, my mind is freed to daydream about God. I wonder about God—God as Redeemer, God as Provider, God as Creator. As the steam fogs up the windows and makes the creases and wrinkles fall away, my heart sings God's praise.

Hallelujah! Give thanks to the LORD because he is good, because his mercy endures forever.

PSALM 106:1
GOD'S WORD

I rejoice to give you thanks and praise,
O God, my Redeemer, Provider, Creator.
Amen.

The Gift of Solitude

I go into my study, shut the door, and leave behind the world of phones and chatter, people and interruptions. My study is a spare bedroom filled with books. A computer on a large glass table occupies the center of the room. A daybed is in one corner; a reading chair is off to one side. In my study, where it's quiet and peaceful, I am free to write or read, think or pray.

I go to my study to find precious solitude. Though I am alone there, I am never truly alone. My study is a sanctuary. In the quiet of my study, regardless of what I may be doing, I am much more aware of God's presence there than in other places.

Very early in the morning,
while it was still dark, Jesus
got up, left the house and
went off to a solitary place,
where he prayed.

MARK 1:35 NIV

Help me to find a little solitude
today, O God, that I may enjoy
Your presence.

Amen.

Put the Kettle On

A scrubbed, gleaming kettle sitting on the stove symbolizes a hospitable home. My kettle is made of steel covered in dark green enamel. It has a steel handle and a chrome lid. When the water boils, the steam plays a little harmonica. My kettle is always ready to boil water to make tea when guests drop by.

Hospitality is the act of entertaining angels unawares. Many times I've found that my guests are the ones who entertain me! By the time the tea is drunk and the cookies consumed, I find that my guests have ministered to me and my needs. I may have served up the tea—but my guests, disguised as angels, served up the sympathy.

Do not forget to entertain strangers, for by so doing some have unwittingly entertained angels.

HEBREWS 13:2 NKJV

O Lord, let me see my guests
clothed in angels' wings.

Amen.

The Art of Finding God

In my study hangs a woodcut of one of Jesus' parables—a woman searching her house for a lost coin. She is looking at the floor, a broom in one hand, a candlestick in the other.

The woodcut and Jesus' parable tell me that the smallest, most ordinary of things have the most value. Like the woman looking for the lost coin, I am to take nothing in my home for granted. I search my home for the things that show forth God's kingdom. My home isn't just a place where I live—it's also where God lives.

"Suppose a woman has ten coins and loses one. Doesn't she light a lamp, sweep the house, and look for the coin carefully until she finds it?"

LUKE 15:8 GOD'S WORD

———— ⚍ ————

Let me find You today,
O God, in the nooks and crannies
and all that is well loved in my home.
Amen.

Home Is Where the Hearth Is

My house has a great fireplace. It's a massive thing built of rose-colored slate. The hearth extends two feet into the room. Two black andirons in the shape of cats hold back the firewood while the light of the fire glows through their hollow eyes.

Winter is a nesting time, a time of going inside with God. I've spent many winter hours with God in front of a roaring fire. With my feet propped up on the big hearth, it's the perfect place to pray and dream of Him. Sometimes I read my Bible; other times I write in my journal. But mostly I sit quietly by the fireside, stare into the fire, and enjoy the warmth of God's love.

"You shall love the LORD your God with all
your heart and with all your soul
and with all your might."

DEUTERONOMY 6:5 NASB

Warm me today, Lord,
with the power of Your love.
Amen.

New Windows

Recently, I replaced all of the old aluminum windows in my home with new double-paned, vinyl-covered frames. What a difference! Not only do the new windows improve the appearance of my home, but the house is also quieter, cleaner (less dust that blows in), warmer in the winter, and cooler in the summer.

Maybe the best part of all is how clean my new windows are—I can look outside and see the world much more clearly. My new, clean windows remind me to keep my own vision clear with faith. When I look at the world through the eyes of faith, I can love instead of judge. I can forgive instead of hold a grudge.

*I will pour out my spirit on all flesh; your
sons and your daughters shall prophesy,
your old men shall dream dreams, and
your young men shall see visions.*

JOEL 2:28 NRSV

—m—

O God, strengthen my faith and let me
see Your world through Your eyes.
Amen.

My Home's Brain

My home's brain is my computer. It sits in my study surrounded by books. I spend a lot of time on the computer—it's a portal to the wide world of information on the Internet; it's a personal shopping mall with my favorite stores; it's a post office connecting me by e-mail to friends and colleagues far away. Most of all, my computer is a sophisticated tablet, a writing tool that helps me to create.

God loves it when we imitate Him by creating something new. I believe God enjoys how I make old words come together in new ways to express the thoughts in my mind and the feelings in my heart.

Therefore, if anyone is in Christ, he is a new creation; old things have passed away; behold, all things have become new.

2 CORINTHIANS 5:17 NKJV

———

Help me to imitate You, O God, and create something new today that gives You pleasure. *Amen.*

Crying in the Shower

Not long ago I came home from a grueling work-week that I had thought would never end. I was stressed out, tired, frustrated, and upset. I decided to take a long, hot shower. As the hot water rained over me, I realized I had to work at least fifteen more years before I could retire. I began to cry. Tears mingled with the water and streamed down my face.

A good cry in the shower is not necessarily sad—I learned that it's one way God heals and restores me. During this difficult time, God used the shower to cleanse me physically, emotionally, and spiritually. Good, clean hot water, a sweet-smelling bar of soap, and warm fluffy towels were God's instruments of healing.

"For you who revere my name, the sun of righteousness will rise with healing in its wings. And you will go out and leap like calves released from the stall."

MALACHI 4:2 NIV

———

O Lord, there is healing in Your wings. Wash away my sadness, and let me know the joy of Your healing presence.

Amen.

Spring on the Patio

Along about the middle of March, I get really tired of winter. Even though the weather is still changeable and too cold for me to enjoy being outside for long, I proclaim mid-March "springtime" on my patio. I go into the garage and drag out the patio furniture—tables, chairs, and a big sun umbrella. I plant spring flowers in the clay flowerpots. I clean and fill the fountain with fresh water, and I roll out the barbecue.

My spring-festooned patio always reminds me that God loves to renew and refresh. I feel as though God has given me a new spirit, a spirit that is young and strong and eager for new things.

You send out your Spirit, and they are
created. You renew the face of the earth.

PSALM 104:30 GOD'SWORD

With You, O God, it is always springtime—
for You send out Your Spirit to all who love You.

Amen.

Setting the Table

When I entertain guests or family, I drape the table with stiffly starched linen. I polish my mother's silverware and set out the good china. I put sparkling crystal stemware at each place. I choose and arrange flowers with care. Finally, I select just the right candlesticks and candles to flank the flowers.

The greatest love is sometimes expressed in the smallest things. God tells me how much He loves me in the smallest of things—a shaft of sunlight pouring through the window on a winter's day, the scent of jasmine coming through an open door. I pay attention to these little things—and pass God's love along when I set the table.

*We're not ashamed to
have this confidence,
because God's love has been
poured into our hearts by
the Holy Spirit, who has been
given to us.*

ROMANS 5:5 GOD'S WORD

Help me to find Your love in the
smallest of things, O God.

Amen.

The Guest Bathroom

My guest bathroom is easily the best room in the house. Last winter, I completely redecorated it with new linoleum, white beaded wainscoting, mint-green wall paint, a shiny chrome medicine cabinet and fixtures, and lovely, gauzy curtains.

A lot of love and care went into making the guest bathroom beautiful. When guests visit my home, I want them to feel as welcome as family. It's a way of sharing God's grace. God has welcomed me into His family by His grace, mercy, and love. By making guests feel welcome, I am sharing a little bit of the grace God has given me.

Each of you as a good manager must use the gift that God has given you to serve others.

1 Peter 4:10 God's Word

May the guests who enter my home, O Lord, find Your welcoming grace.

Amen.

Tokens of Love

There's a certain home-improvement warehouse store I love to spend time—and money—in. Walking through its aisles, pushing one of those giant-size shopping carts, I'm dazzled by things that can improve my home. I feel that I can do anything and that the possibilities are endless. Only my imagination and my budget limit me.

I love my home more than any other place on earth. The tools and materials I lug home from the warehouse store each weekend are tokens of my love. From the gardens to the gutters, from the windows to the wainscoting, my home is covered in symbols of God's love.

You are like a building that was built on the foundation of the apostles and prophets. Christ Jesus himself is the most important stone in that building.

EPHESIANS 2:20 NCV

O God, fill my home with Your loving presence today.

Amen.

A Garden Cure

I am not a naturally calm person. I've got lots of nervous energy, and I worry easily about silly, meaningless things. I've found that my garden offers a cure for anxiety. The feel of the sunshine, the fresh smell of the air and the earth, the fragrance of the flowers, and the vivid brilliance of all the colors create an oasis of serenity.

No wonder Jesus pointed to flowers when He told His followers to stop worrying. I've only to look at the flowers in my garden to be assured of God's providence. When I start to fret and worry need-lessly, I grab my pruning shears and head for the garden—and know the grace of God.

"Why do you worry about clothes? Look at how the lilies in the field grow. They don't work or make clothes for themselves. But I tell you that even Solomon with his riches was not dressed as beautifully as one of these flowers."

MATTHEW 6:28-29 NCV

—⌇—

I will look at the flowers and not worry today, O God, because I know You will take care of me.

Amen.

Homes Have Hearts

Homes have hearts. My home has three—my cats. Nothing beats coming home after a hard day at work, turning the key in the lock, and hearing a chorus of meows on the other side of the door. The sight of a cat curled up sleeping on a pillow, his head turned under with one paw covering his eyes, instantly calms and soothes me. And when the cats tear around the house, I hoot with laughter.

My cats are living reminders to me to take care of my own soul, to nurture my soul with prayer, to give my soul plenty of time in the light of God's love, and to encourage my soul to be grateful to God for all His mercies—especially for cats.

Create in me a clean heart, O God; and renew a right spirit within me.

PSALM 51:10 KJV

Let me be ever mindful
of my soul's needs,
O God, that You may renew
a right spirit
within me.
Amen.

The Garage

Over the years my garage got so full of junk and unused stuff that I could hardly get one car inside. In my garage I had crammed an exercise machine, two broken lamps, a big box fan, more than a dozen cans of paint, boxes my computer was shipped in, and at least two dozen old garden pots. Things were falling off the shelves and hanging from the rafters. Finally, I had a big garage sale, and now I can walk from the car to the house, my eyes open wide, my head held high.

God loves simplicity. He wants me to live my life uncluttered by unnecessary items that could distract me from Him, my true first Love. My garage sale helped me to simplify my life, to see what was really right, pure, and admirable. In a sense, my garage sale helped me to see God more clearly.

Finally, brothers, whatever is true, whatever is noble,
whatever is right, whatever is pure, whatever is lovely,
whatever is admirable—if anything is excellent or
praiseworthy—think about such things.

PHILIPPIANS 4:8 NIV

Show me how to simplify my life, O God, so
that I may never lose sight of You.

Amen.

A Rainy Day on the Couch

Most of the time, the sun shines in California. Rainy season doesn't kick in here until January, and it lasts until April, sometimes as late as May. Then it's over for the rest of the year.

I like rainy days because they give me a meteorological excuse to lie on the couch and daydream about God. It's as though God has granted me permission to stop being busy and instead stretch out on the couch with a cup of tea, my Bible, and my journal and meditate about how good He has been to me. I read a little, sip a little tea, and write a bit. I'm overwhelmed by how good this life is and how much God has blessed me.

*I will meditate on all Your work And
muse on Your deeds.*

PSALM 77:12 NASB

May there be time today, O Lord, to
sit quietly on the couch and dream
of You.

Amen.

Bedtime

There comes an evening sometime in autumn when the frost is definitely on the pumpkin. That's when I take my flannel sheets out of their summer storage and put them on the bed. With the covers pulled up to my chin, the feeling of warmth and comfort is indescribable.

The life of faith is a little like bedtime on a cool autumn night. The life of faith is trusting in God for everything. Trusting in God feels like rest to me; my whole soul relaxes in His grace. When I am troubled or confronted with one of life's problems, I trust God. I send my soul to rest in His love and mercy. I trust Him with whatever troubles me.

*"Don't let your hearts be troubled.
Trust in God, and trust in me."*

JOHN 14:1 NCV

Let me know, O Lord, the sublime rest
and comfort that comes from
trusting You with my whole life.
Amen.

The Spare Room

I turned the spare room in my house into a hobby room. I set up a table with my sewing machine and embroidery chest. I set up—permanently—my ironing board and iron. I placed my orchids on special plant shelves in the room. Then, I set up my exercise machine and put a television in front of it. Now I can indulge in my hobbies of sewing, orchid cultivation, or exercising without wasting time setting up.

God wants us to enjoy life. Work is important, but it's not everything. When I'm busy with one of my hobbies, I find it's so much easier to praise God and thank Him for all good gifts. My troubles slip away, and my being is flooded with the knowledge that God is very good.

Thou wilt shew me the path of life: in thy presence is fulness of joy; at thy right hand there are pleasures for evermore.

PSALM 16:11 KJV

O God, help me to take
the time to enjoy this
life You have given me
so that I may rejoice in
You more.
Amen.

The Birdbath

A wall-sized window in my living room over-looks the front garden. In the middle of this garden is a stone birdbath. Finches, sparrows, cedar waxwings (in winter), juncos, California towhees, and robins are frequent bathers. When not bathing, the birds delicately perch on the side of the birdbath and sip the water.

As I watch them bathe, I think of Jesus' teaching about the sparrows. If God so loves the birds, how much more must He love me! I know that God will give me whatever I need. He holds me in the palm of His hand, and I am at peace.

"Look at the birds in the air. They don't
plant or harvest or store food in barns,
but your heavenly Father feeds them.
And you know that you are worth much
more than the birds."

MATTHEW 6:26 NCV

I have nothing to worry about today, O God, because I
know that You will give me all that I need.

Amen.

Cooking as Prayer

I love to cook for and entertain family and friends. The preparation is as much fun as the actual event. I put my favorite music on the stereo and go to work—chopping, stirring, blending, baking, stewing, sautéing, simmering.

For me, cooking is a way to "pray without ceasing." It is a wordless prayer that comes straight from the heart as an act of love. As I mince the garlic, add the salt, or whisk the cream, I think of those I love sitting down to the dinner I'm preparing, and my heart is filled with gratitude to God. My gratitude takes the shape of casseroles and cakes, soups and salads, roasts and ratatouilles.

Rejoice evermore. Pray without ceasing.
In every thing give thanks: for this is
the will of God in Christ Jesus
concerning you.

1 THESSALONIANS 5:16-18 KJV

—m—

I rejoice to give You thanks and praise
without ceasing, O God.
Amen.

My Closet

My home has lots of closets. One day while organizing and cleaning, I found my mother's two-foot-long, black patent-leather purse from the early sixties. As I held Mom's purse, I could faintly smell her perfume. Instantly I was a little girl again watching her get ready to go out. Though she had died several years earlier, suddenly I missed her terribly.

Then I realized that God was using my memories to comfort me—to help keep my mother alive for me. I also realized that she is with Him now, and I was deeply consoled and comforted by the promise that I will see her again in Heaven.

As the sufferings of Christ
abound in us, so our
consolation also abounds
through Christ.

2 CORINTHIANS 1:5 NKJV

—⁂—

Thank you, O God,
for the comfort and
consolation of
memories.
Amen.

Dining In

One of the things I like best about my home is its formal dining room. A room dedicated exclusively to dining lets me focus on the loved ones gathered to share a meal. The dining room is particularly beautiful in the evening at dinnertime—the red walls glow by candlelight, and the effect is intimate and cozy. Dining with those I love is an act of love.

Sometimes I think of Jesus' Last Supper, upstairs in a separate, cozy dining room. It wasn't a sad event; it was a special time for Jesus to share the Passover meal with those He loved. In those few special hours Jesus focused on His loved ones. All distractions lay elsewhere.

The disciples went out and came to the city, and found it just as He had told them; and they prepared the Passover. When it was evening He came with the twelve.

MARK 14:16-17 NASB

—⁓—

O Lord, help me to see each
mealtime as an act of love.

Amen.

Kitchen Hospitality

I have an eat-in kitchen, and I entertain family and friends in the warmth and intimacy of it. I like to transform guests into friends by bringing them into the kitchen as I put the finishing touches on a meal. I sit them down at the kitchen table, pour them a beverage, and offer them hors d'oeuvres; then we laugh and talk until dinner is ready.

Hospitality is an act of love, an act of faith. The whole point of hospitality is to transform strangers into friends. Through Christ, we who were once strangers are made into God's friends. And because I know God's friendship, I extend that friendship to my guests.

Be joyful because you have hope. Be patient
when trouble comes, and pray at all times.
Share with God's people who need help.
Bring strangers in need into your homes.

ROMANS 12:12-13 NCV

—᷍᷍᷍—

May all who enter my kitchen,
O God, find love, laughter, and You.
Amen.

The Attic

Once in a while I have to journey to my attic to find something I stored there. I don't look forward to going. The attic is cold in winter and hot in summer; it's filled with an incredible amount of junk; and it's dark. When I find what I'm looking for, however, I'm so glad that I didn't throw it out; relief and happiness are my rewards.

Taking a good look at my soul is sometimes like taking a trip to the attic. Once in a while I have to wade through some of the junk I've let accumulate in my soul in order to find God's forgiveness. It's not always pleasant, but it is always rewarding. I offer up grudges or unloving thoughts in search of God's forgiveness.

"When you are praying, first forgive anyone you are holding a grudge against, so that your Father in heaven will forgive your sins, too."

MARK 11:25 NLT

—⟆⟇—

Help me to forgive those who have wronged me, O God, that I might find Your mercy and forgiveness.

Amen

The Litter Box

I pamper my three cats shamelessly with boutique cat food. I give them the complete run of the house in which they can chase the latest in cat toys. I let them take up as much of my bed as they want while I balance precariously on the edge. I show my greatest love for them, however, when I clean their litter boxes. That stinky, messy, very unpleasant chore is pure love in action.

When I look around, I can see how much God loves me. Even when I have been unpleasant and given hurt instead of love, God's love leaps into action with forgiveness and mercy. God promises to love me forever no matter how unlovely I behave. And I feel His love all the more.

Therefore, as God's chosen people,
holy and dearly loved, clothe yourselves
with compassion, kindness, humility,
gentleness and patience.

COLOSSIANS 3:12 NIV

I know Your love more keenly, O God,
when You touch me with Your mercy.
Amen.

A Long, Hot Soak

I pull the car into the garage after a long, life-threatening, Friday-evening commute. My shoulders are tied in knots; my neck feels like a steel brace. I'm as relaxed as a tightly wound coil. There's only one thing to do—take a long, hot soak in the tub.

I slip into fragrant bubbles, letting their scent and the heat of the water work their magic. I pretend a bubble is a worry I've been holding on to all week, and I pop it, releasing the trouble into Jesus' care. Slowly, my worries fade, and I begin to daydream about God. Worry becomes impossible. It is enough to float softly into God's arms, removed from care.

"Do not worry about tomorrow; for tomorrow will care for itself. Each day has enough trouble of its own."

MATTHEW 6:34 NASB

Bless the water in my tub, O Lord,
and wash all my worries away with
the warmth of Your touch.

Amen.

Spring Cleaning

For most people, spring means flowers and baby animals and soft breezes. For me, it means five different kinds of cleansers, two mops (one for tile, one for hardwood), a cobweb duster, an array of sponges, rubber gloves, and two buckets of hot water.

Spring cleaning is a great expression of hope. Hope is the expectation of joyfully sharing God's glory. When I scrub off winter's dirt and grime, I expect to see a little bit of God's glory shining through my home. I look at my freshly polished house and think that this is what Heaven will be like—all will be bright and clean, shot through with the dazzling power and light of God's glory. And I will be finally, completely home.

*Because of our faith, Christ has brought us
into this place of highest privilege where we
now stand, and we confidently and joyfully
look forward to sharing God's glory.*

ROMANS 5:2 NLT

—⁂—

When I clean my home, O
God, help me to find a little
bit of Your glory.

Amen.

Words

On my desk in my study I keep a bowl full of words, each accompanied by a drawing of an angel that illustrates its meaning. So the word *harmony* has a picture of a choir of angels singing; *patience* has an angel quietly knitting; *surrender* has an angel holding up a white flag.

I am a professional writer. My home is filled with written words and spoken words. Words can wound as well as heal. So I take care to make sure the words that fill my house, the words that I write and say, tell of God's love and mercy.

In the beginning was the Word, and the Word was with God, and the Word was God.

JOHN 1:1 NRSV

O Lord, help me to be mindful of my words today. When I speak, let others hear Your love.
Amen.

Plumbing

When the building inspector announced that my soon-to-be new home had copper plumbing, I was thrilled. However, even copper pipes get plugged up and need the ministrations of a plumber. I quickly learned that there's nothing I could do if my plumbing wasn't working.

My latest plumbing problem showed me how much more heartfelt my prayers are when a crisis comes upon me. My everyday prayers often lack the urgency and passion that come easily when the plumbing is backed up. My life is prayer to God—and my everyday prayers should be just as powerful and as passionate as my prayers in times of trouble.

Through each day the LORD pours his unfailing love upon me, and through each night I sing his songs, praying to God who gives me life.

PSALMS 42:8 NLT

O God, my life is a prayer to You.
Let my prayer be filled with
passion and power every day.

Amen.

The Fountain

One day my father surprised my mother with a large garden fountain—a statue of a homely peasant girl holding a bucket, pouring water into two big shell basins. It sat next to their back door, burbling away for years. After my mother died, my dad asked me to take the fountain. Now the fountain sits just outside my back door, burbling away.

While the fountain may not be that attractive, it makes the most beautiful sound. Everything seems fresher, newer, and prettier to the music of falling water. My fountain tells me that God still moves across the face of the waters, no matter where those waters are. When my fountain plays, I know that God walks in my garden in the cool of the day.

The earth was empty, a formless mass cloaked in darkness. And the Spirit of God was hovering over its surface.

GENESIS 1:2 NLT

The sound of water, O Lord, tells me that You move across Your world with love and mercy.

Amen.

Living on a Fault Line

My house is built about ten feet away from one of the most famous earthquake faults in the world—the Hayward Fault. The Hayward Fault plows right through one of the most densely populated regions of the Bay Area, where geologists predict a one-in-three chance of a major, devastating earthquake to strike within thirty years.

The Hayward Fault teaches me not to take God's mercy for granted. Every second of every day that the fault doesn't move is an act of His mercy and care. God—and God alone—allows my world to continue. I praise and thank Him for my beautiful home in this lovely city by the Bay.

Now GOD, don't hold out on me, don't hold back your passion. Your love and truth are all that keeps me together.

PSALM 40:11 THE MESSAGE

O Lord, You—and You alone—sustain my world with Your great mercy. Thank You for each precious moment, O God.
Amen.

The Ship's Clock

My father repairs and restores old, key-wound clocks. My home has several clocks that dad has restored and given to me. My favorite is a brass ship's clock. It makes the most beautiful sound—it rings a bell telling the hour of the watch. I can always tell exactly what time it is just by listening to my ship's clock ringing out the watch.

The older I get, the more wakeful I become in the middle of the night. I lie in bed and listen for the ship's clock to tell me the watch. I meditate on God in the night watches, and I am constantly aware of His loving presence.

When I remember You on my bed, I meditate on You in the night watches.

PSALM 63:6 NASB

—⟋⟍—

I meditate on You in the night watches,
O God, and can feel Your loving presence
watching over me.

Amen.

Home Improvements

I'm a big believer in home improvement. I almost always have a project going on or am saving money to finance another home improvement in the future. It never stops—new landscaping, new windows, new gutters, new paint, new tile. I take a long-term view. Home improvements are an investment in the future.

I take a long-term view of the life of faith too. God wants me to love and value today—but to hope passionately for the future. He wants me to keep my feet on the ground and my eyes fixed on Heaven. It's like my home improvements—everything I do in faith today has value one day in Heaven.

*Through him you have come to trust
in God, who raised him from the
dead and gave him glory, so that
your faith and hope are set on God.*

1 PETER 1:21 NRSV

Thank you for today and
all it brings, O Lord, and thank
You for the place You prepare for
me in Heaven.

Amen.

Chores

Every homeowner has chores—garbage to take
out, gardens to tend and water, home repairs
to make, laundry to wash, dishes to do, meals
to cook. Then there's the cleaning, mopping,
scrubbing, dusting, and polishing. I get tired
just writing about all the chores that need
doing.

But I have a secret to making chores more
enjoyable. In my study I have a quote from
Esther de Waal hanging on the wall: "She has
made the mundane the edge of glory." I try to
perform each chore as if I am doing it for God.
Then my chores become acts of worship, and
they become expressions of my love.

We, who with unveiled faces all reflect the Lord's glory, are being transformed into his likeness with ever-increasing glory, which comes from the Lord, who is the Spirit.

2 CORINTHIANS 3:18 NIV

—⁂—

Bless the chores I do today, O God, that I might bring You honor and glory and give you all of my love.

Amen.

Peace and Quiet

When I lived in apartments, I could always hear my neighbors—doors slamming, people chatting, cars coming and going, televisions blaring. The best part of homeownership for me has been the peace and quiet.

Silence is my home's gift to me. After a hard day at the office, the peace and quiet of my home is like a soothing balm. The healing power of silence makes it possible for me to hear God. In silence I can listen for His gentle whisper without noisy distractions. And in that holy silence, I find rest and happiness.

I have stilled and quieted myself, just as a small child is quiet with its mother. Yes, like a small child is my soul within me.

PSALM 131:2 NLT

In this quiet moment, O God, let me hear Your gentle whisper.

Amen.

House Hunting

House hunting is quite an adventure. After I sold my first home, I looked for weeks before I found my present home. I'd lost the bid on yet another house when my agent suggested I look at just one more. A fifties split-level ranch wasn't what I was looking for, but I took one look and fell in love.

The life of faith is a lot like house hunting. It takes patience and perseverance. It takes a willingness to be constantly surprised by the love of God. When you least expect it, you will experience God's love in the smile of a friend or in the radiance of His glory shining through the clouds after a storm.

Let patience have its perfect work,
that you may be perfect and complete,
lacking nothing.

JAMES 1:4 NKJV

O Lord, help me to be patient with You.
Let me be surprised by joy one day soon.

Amen.

The Guest Room

I have a room that's always ready. It has a bed piled with a fluffy down comforter and big pillows, a writing desk in the corner filled with paper and pens, a comfy chair with a footstool by the bedside, a chest of drawers with a pair of clean pajamas and a warm terry bathrobe. I've made it cheery and comfortable, warm and inviting. It's my guest room, and it's always ready for guests, planned or unplanned.

I try to keep my heart as ready as my guest room. I never know when to expect God. I do not know the hour or day when God will knock on my heart's door, His arms full of grace.

"Say to the owner of the house, 'The Teacher asks you, "Where is the guest room, where I may eat the Passover with my disciples?"' He will show you a large room upstairs, already furnished. Make preparations for us there."

LUKE 22:11-12 NRSV

Give me a ready and
willing heart, O God,
to greet You with joy
when You come.
Amen.

The Kitchen Garden

I grow an herb garden in my backyard, a few short steps from the kitchen, and it teaches me the power of small plants. Oregano, basil, dill, chives, thyme, cilantro, and garlic— just a little bit of any one of these plants can flavor whole meals. The flavors of these herbs are highly concentrated, and whether I dry them or snip them fresh, just a little goes a long way.

Similarly, the power of faith is often concentrated in small things. The kingdom of Heaven is like a mustard seed. If I can cultivate just a little faith deep in my heart, I can expect great things: I can love the unlovable; I can forgive the unforgivable; I can walk through the darkness.

"The kingdom of heaven is like a mustard seed that someone took and sowed in his field."

MATTHEW 13:31 NRSV

With my faith in You, O God,
I can expect great things.
Amen.

The Roof

I had my house professionally inspected before I bought it. The inspector climbed and crawled all over the house for more than three hours. Then he delivered his report—the roof was not only made of the finest roofing material, it was also perfectly installed. "This roof," he said, "will long outlast you."

Just as my perfectly installed roof protects me from the elements—the sun, the wind, and the rain—God protects me under the shadow of His wings. On a dark, rainy night I lie snug and dry in bed and give thanks for my roof. I imagine myself snug underneath God's wings, as well, and know that I am protected from darkness and fear.

*Keep me as the apple of the eye,
hide me under the shadow of
thy wings.*

Psalm 17:8 KJV

O God, let me lie under the shadow of
Your wings now and forever.

 Amen.

The Forty-Six-Year-Old Rose Bush

I have an enormous, forty-six-year-old rose bush in my backyard. My elderly neighbor tells me it was planted when the house was built. When I first moved in it was seven feet high and eight feet wide. It has a gnarled, branching trunk. Every summer it produces gorgeous, deep-red velvet roses the size of salad plates. It must have a tremendously deep root system that goes to the center of the earth. That root system must have sustained the rose bush through years of neglect before I moved in.

Faith in God is like my bush's root system—a boundless stream that sustains and nurtures me. I can weather anything when I sink my roots as deeply into God as I can.

He shall be like a tree
planted by the waters, Which
spreads out its roots by the
river, And will not fear when
heat comes; But its leaf will
be green, And will not be
anxious in the year of
drought, Nor
will cease from yielding fruit.

JEREMIAH 17:8 NKJV

O Lord, I am like a tree whose roots sink
deep into the river. I can face anything
because of my faith in You.
Amen.

Neighborhood Watch

My city of Oakland invented the popular Neighborhood Watch program, in which neighbors watch out for each other and report suspicious or criminal activity in their neighborhoods. Reducing crime is only one benefit of the program. Even better benefits are that people get to know their neighbors and that the neighborhood turns into a caring community.

I think of the Church as a kind of Neighborhood Watch program. As a member of a church, I watch out for other believers, and other believers watch out for me. We take care of each other, and together, we watch for the coming of the Lord.

"Keep awake therefore, for you do not know on what day your Lord is coming."

Help me to take care of my neighbors, O Lord, and help us to be alert and watch out for You.
Amen.

Oil Lamps

I collect oil lamps and display them throughout my home—brass ones, pewter ones, and glass ones. I light my lamps mostly during the winter, when the days are short and the nights are long. Their warm glow is cheerful, and they emit a light scent of kerosene, a homey smell I love. I also love the shadows the oil lamps cast. The shadows dance outside the glow of the lamps, big against the walls and curtains.

I burn my oil lamps in winter to remind me of the true Light of the World, who shines so brightly in the darkness. I sit in the winter's lamplight warmed by the knowledge that God's presence lights my way.

"I am the light of the world. Whoever follows me will never walk in darkness but will have the light of life."

JOHN 8:12 NRSV

You are the Light of the World, O Lord. May I ever walk by Your light.

Amen.

My Town

There is so much about my hometown of Oakland, California, that is truly beautiful, pleasant, and good. Like a lot of big urban cities, however, it's not always an easy place to love. We have more than our share of crime, troubled schools, and poverty, but we are trying hard to fight these evils and make Oakland a better place. It's working.

My house sits on an Oakland hillside. From a second-floor bedroom window, I can peek through the trees and see the lights of downtown. The light of God shines over my city, and His light can never be put out.

Ye are the light of the world.
A city that is set on
an hill cannot be hid.

MATTHEW 5:14 KJV

———

O God, let Your light shine
on my hometown and make us
a city set on a hill that
declares Your love.

Amen.

Coming Home

As the garage door slowly opens, I feel relieved, happy, warm, and just plain good to be home again. There's nothing like the feeling of pulling into my garage after a long day at work.

The welcome I feel driving into my garage is a little bit of what I believe I'll feel at the threshold of Heaven. As Heaven's gates swing slowly open, there will be a tremendous, over-powering sense of welcome. God will welcome me home, beckoning me to come inside to find deep, profound joy in His kingdom. Inside there will be laughter and singing and happiness without end.

*Therefore, my brothers, be all the more eager
to make your calling and election sure.
For if you do these things, you will never fall,
and you will receive a rich welcome into the
eternal kingdom of our Lord and
Savior Jesus Christ.*

2 PETER 1:10-11 NIV

—⚂—

I love to feel Your welcome,
O God, the warmth of Your smile,
the love in Your arms.

Amen.